IMAGES
of America

ANTIOCH

The Hiram Buttrick Sawmill is the most recognized image of Antioch. The original mill was built along Sequoit Creek in 1839 by an early pioneer, Hiram Buttrick. The sawmill, along with a steam gristmill that was built by John H. Elliott in 1856, was the center around which the village would emerge. In 1976, while the Bicentennial Committee was working on projects for the nation's 200th birthday, the idea was born to build a working replica of the sawmill. It was donated and built by more than a thousand people of Antioch, and in 1978, it was completed and dedicated. There is a time capsule buried on the site that will be raised in 2076.

On the cover: Taken on July 3 (believed to be in 1908), this photograph shows the town in preparation for the big celebration the next day. The Fourth of July has been a major holiday in Antioch since its beginnings in the 1840s. This is a photograph by Ray Lugar, who was well known in this area for the extensive work he did. Lugar was in this area between 1906 and 1918 and took photographs from the town out to the resorts. Thank you, Ray Lugar, for preserving this time in Antioch. (Courtesy of the Lake Region Historical Society.)

IMAGES
of America

ANTIOCH

Wendy Maston and Robin Kessell

ARCADIA
PUBLISHING

Published by Arcadia Publishing
Charleston SC, Chicago IL, Portsmouth NH, San Francisco CA

Library of Congress Catalog Card Number: 2007924697

For all general information contact Arcadia Publishing at:
Telephone 843-853-2070
Fax 843-853-0044
E-mail sales@arcadiapublishing.com
For customer service and orders:
Toll-Free 1-888-313-2665

Visit us on the Internet at www.arcadiapublishing.com

CONTENTS

ACKNOWLEDGMENTS

This book is the culmination of years of collecting the history of Antioch. In 1992, members of the Lakes Region Historical Society (LRHS) put together a book *Pictorial History of Antioch, 1892–1992*. It was because of the hours of hard work, sifting through hundreds of old papers and repairing photographs, that they put together a wonderful book for the community. To that group of people thank-you is not enough. We are forever grateful.

Thank-you must also go to others who have written articles and booklets that have come into the collections of the LRHS. Many of these have no specific author given but one was written by the late Roberta Selter Knirsch. Roberta was a major force in the early days of the society and spent hours recording all the artifacts that were donated to the museum. She wrote a booklet called, *The Town of Antioch, Its First Hundred Years, 1837–1937*. (The booklet is available at the LRHS.)

Two other members of LRHS that had input into this book are Art Doty and Pam Martz. Both are very knowledgeable and answered dozens of questions.

A major thank-you goes to Ainsley Brook Wonderling. Ainsley is our museum director and possibly knows more about Antioch and its families than anyone else. Her devotion to preserving the history of this town is surpassed by no one. When she did not know the answer to a question she knew who did. Thank you, Ainsley.

Another special thank-you goes to Thomas and Catherine (Bogan) Middlebrook. Tom has an extensive postcard collection of Antioch and the surrounding area. He allowed us to browse through that collection where we found many wonderful images of Antioch that were not in the museum collection. Those images are individually identified within the book. All images not identified are from the LRHS collections.

To all the members of the society who answered questions at meetings, on the street, or over the phone, we are forever grateful. We must not let the rich history of Antioch ever be forgotten. We must always be "Preserving the past to educate the future."

INTRODUCTION

While doing the research for this book, we came across a narrative at the Antioch Public District Library. Prepared by the pupils and teachers of the Antioch Grade School in 1918, it gives an early history of our beautiful "little" town. Read *History of Antioch*, prepared by the pupils and teachers of the Antioch Grade School District No. 34, of Lake County in 1918, and try to imagine what life was like back then:

> Back in York State in 1835, when the first frosts had caressed the landscape and the answering blush was everywhere to be seen, three men Thomas Gage, Thomas Warner and W. B. Gage, sound, sturdy, robust: occasionally met and talked about the great and wonderful "West." They chatted about the "Illinois Country," where the large game was still plentiful; the deer, the wolf, the buffalo; where the fishing was good and the wild birds' myriad, where the black soil was deep and rich and where farms might be had for the taking.

The lands that we know as Illinois and Wisconsin had been opened to white settlers by the government in the mid-1830s. Many adventurous pioneers chose to take advantage of this with the hope of improving their lives. Although we do not know the details of the trip of the men who founded our area it was known that men would walk with their meager belongings until they came to the Ohio River where they would join others.

> Joining themselves to a flat boat company they floated down the majestic river. How wonderful must have been their voyage—days of enchantment and nights of mystic witchery!! Those nights when they silently stood sentinel over their sleeping companions, when the river seemed like a ribbon of silver in the moonlight, when the laugh of the loon or the call of the owl from the deep dark shadows on either densely wooded bank might mean "Indians!"

After a long and dangerous journey the men arrived in the small settlement of Chicago sometime in the fall of 1836. Traveling north they found the beautiful area with a creek they later named Sequoit. The Gage brothers built a log cabin on the site where Antioch Village Hall now stands. Thomas Warner built his log cabin on the west shore of Loon Lake, about two miles away, and then traveled with the Gages to Milwaukee, Wisconsin, to welcome other early settlers. There they rendezvoused with Joseph Ingalls, Miles Shepard and his wife Eliza Ann Gage Shepard, Myron Stevens, and others who had been convinced to travel to the Great Lakes upon the "slow sailing vessels of that time."

The small party rejoiced in each others company and then returned to the site of the Gage settlement to build their own log cabins. "With no nails, no shingles, no planed boards and no glass were the cabins built," the 1918 account informs us. "And soon all was cozy and snug." The pioneers became fast friends with the local Native Americans. They spent the winter months felling trees, fishing, and hunting the plentiful wild game.

Over the next few years more people came. Although the area was not the best for farming as it was considered somewhat swampy, it offered so many other wonderful things that many chose to stay instead of moving on.

In 1838, Hiram Buttrick built a sawmill on Sequoit Creek and the Gage brothers erected a large, low log-house hotel. A general store was opened by Mr. Head. In 1839, there were two blacksmith shops for the three horses and the single one-horse wagon of the settlement! The same year Mr. Ring erected a building for a store—the King Drug Store now occupies this same building. Two frame houses were built and four new log cabins. The settlers got their mail from Waukegan. A carrier made the round trip each week. Later a railroad ran through Wadsworth and mail was then distributed each day. Mr. F. F. Munson conducted a general store and permitted the upper unfinished room to be used for school purposes. Welcome Jilson was the first teacher and he had one pupil, Thomas Gage.

The store referenced above as the King Drug Store is the property that now houses the Escape Nail Shop, Decano's, and Infini-Tea in downtown Antioch.

The first church service was held in Mr. Shepard's barn. Mr. Shepard was a very religious man and he wanted the settlement to have a Biblical name. Jericho and Joppa were suggested; Gage Settlement and Bristol were warmly advocated. Finally a day was set upon which a vote would be taken. Some wag suggested Antioch as both unique and ancient. The majority was decidedly for Antioch. At the time of the naming of Antioch land was worth $1.25 per acre and wages were 50 cents a day. The first town meeting was held in 1844. The village form of government was adopted February 29th, 1892. The first doctors to come to the village were Dr. Leroy Gage and Dr. Salisbury.

The group had tried to form the town government early in the 1860s but the majority did not want any formal government at that time. It took until 1892 for the town to officially become a village. Incorporation came on February 29, 1892.

The beautiful lakes near Antioch were a favorite camping ground. The wooded shores, where game was abundant, the broad expanses of laughing water, where fish and wild fowl flourished and the silent burial mounds of his forefathers, made this a sacred spot to the Indian. Today it is not an uncommon thing for farmers to turn up with the plough, stone hatchets, beads, arrow heads of all sizes, and even Indian skulls and moldy bones.

In the early 1900s, when building increased, all the above mentioned items actually became a nuisance to the workers. The abundance proved that this had been a major meeting place for the Native American tribes. Some of these items, including a mortar and pestle found by Solomon La Plant while plowing his field, can be seen at the Lakes Region Historical Society's School House Museum at the corner of Depot and Main Streets.

Antioch, today, is a quiet little village of nearly 1000 inhabitants. From May until October, it is the center of a flourishing summer resort business. Many people of refinement and wealth have cottages where the Indians once camped. Thousands of workers spend their vacations at the large hotels which are to be found on all of the lakes. These all came to Antioch on the Soo Line and are soon whizzed to their destination by the "universal car." Hunters and fishermen visit the lakes in the Spring and Fall. During the Winter business is at a standstill, waiting the magic breath of Spring. The lotus beds at Grass Lake are famous. Pickerel, bass, and sunfish are found in all the lakes. The Great Spirit whispers through wood and across lake—"Come and rest."

Today the village and the surrounding area are home to thousands of people all year around. The winter is as active as all the other seasons. The lotus beds are returning after being almost destroyed, fishing is still good, and the train still passes by.

This was quite a vivid description, including insights from the people of almost a century ago. These images and stories are but a few of the hundreds in the archives of the museum. Our new center, the Lasco Archive Center, at 965 Main Street, will open to the public in the fall of 2007.

This "bird's-eye view of Antioch," around 1910, was taken from the top of the stand pipe that was built in 1907. The bottom right is the Grice Hotel. On the left is the United Methodist Church. Above the church is the schoolhouse, and in the center is the feed mill that processed the farmers' goods well into the 1950s. A train moves along the track in the background. The white building at the end of the street on the right is the Antioch News (see page 55).

One

THOSE THAT CAME

The children are the hope and future of any community. The reason that these young people have gathered is unknown and only one name is known. Helen Nabor is the young lady in the third row farthest to the left. Perhaps this was a May Day celebration as there are lily of the valley flowers on the table. The young ladies are very pretty in their dresses and hair bows. The young gentlemen do not appear to be dressed for play. Whatever the occasion, it is certain that it was important. The explorers, farmers, businessmen, doctors, and others came and settled by their own choice. The children had to follow. Whether these children had followed their parents from another place or were born here, Antioch became their home. And some of them grew up to be leaders of the community and became a part of history.

This magnificent home was built around 1875. It was home to Daniel A. Williams's family and stood until the bulldozer took it down in 1972. The Heritage Building (800 North Main Street) is on this location now. From left to right are Addie Williams, an unidentified visiting cousin, Laura Williams, Aunt Elsie Williams (standing), the housekeeper, baby Ruth Williams in the buggy, and Ray Williams.

John C. James was one of the influential men in town. He had a furniture store and was the undertaker for some time. He began construction on this home in 1888 and finished it within the year. It stood on the property that is now the southeast corner of Orchard Street and Toft Avenue.

Contractor Hugh G. Dardis built this home for his family. His company also built the 1892 schoolhouse at Main Street and Depot Street. (Home to the Lakes Region Historical Society.) From left to right are Hugh G. Dardis, Anna Dardis (sitting), neighbor Mrs. Ames (sitting), Elsie Dardis, Gertie Smart, and Don Dardis with the horse. This location is now 425 Lake Street (Chase Bank).

Solomon La Plant was an early resident of Antioch. His company did masonry work, and they were involved in the building of an addition, in 1900, to the schoolhouse and of the first stand pipe in 1907. This photograph shows Solomon with baby Letha. The La Plant name is still known around Antioch.

The Proctor cabin was located off Trevor Road near North Avenue. This photograph was taken around 1886. From left to right are Murry Horton, Lydia Proctor Horton, Eddie Proctor (Lydia's brother), Eunice Proctor (mother), Sophia Graves (Eunice's sister), Carrie Graves (Sophia's daughter), Norris Proctor (Lydia's oldest brother), Cyrus Proctor (father), Ira Simons, Martha Proctor (married to Hiram Proctor) with baby Ira, and Jack Drury.

Families were important and group photographs valued. When the traveling photographer arrived before 1908, members gathered together. Here are both the Osmond and James families. From left to right are (first row) Joseph James Sr., Martha Howdan James, William James, Lester Osmond Sr., and William Harrison Osmond; (second row) Bertha James Gilbert, Joseph C. James Jr., two unidentified women, and Ida James Osmond. The old Native American relic in the photograph was found on the farm, but its whereabouts today is unknown.

Myron and Sarah (Shepard) Stevens were the in-laws of Elijah Simmons. Both were born in the 1780s and were children of Revolutionary War soldiers. They came with the family groups to the Antioch area in 1841. Myron purchased 160 acres of land at $1.25 per acre. Sarah passed away in 1855 and Myron in 1859.

Elijah Simmons was born on January 26, 1803, in New York State and orphaned at an early age. After completing an apprenticeship he married and, along with his in-laws and other family members, came to the Antioch area in 1841. In early 1850, he left the family and made his way to the gold fields of California. He died in Hangtown, California, on December 22, 1850, never having made his fortune.

A very typical 1880s family, the Emmons were important in the early days of Antioch. The girls married names are given in parentheses. From left to right are mother Sara Ham Emmons, Alice, Artenessa (Grice), and father Rockwell Dean Emmons with Callie (La Plant) seated in front. Sarah and Rockwell celebrated their 60th anniversary on November 16, 1919. Callie later died in childbirth at a very young age.

Dr. Winsor Warriner, born in 1874, was a true country doctor. He came to the area as a young doctor when the area was still considered backwoods. By the time this picture was taken in Antioch in 1908, he was a well respected member of the community. He made his rounds with horse and buggy and visited all the farmers in the outlaying areas. In later years, he would continue those rounds in an automobile.

A common summer event would be to take a hayride. This photograph shows the Wertz family on the Morley Farm on Trevor Road around 1915. Although the order is unknown, the following people are on the wagon: Clayton and Frieda Wertz; Mr. and Mrs. Augustus Singer (parents of Frieda Wertz); Charles, Wesley, and Arthur Wertz; and Mr. and Mrs. Harry Larson.

The Palmer family home was on North Avenue and had to be a whirlwind of activity. Imagine having six sons and no daughters to help around the house. Mary was a lucky lady to have all six of her sons survive into manhood. Sitting next to her is her husband Walter. Behind them from left to right are Fred, John, Harry, George, Edwin, and Frank.

The Antioch Brass Band could be heard at the Opera House or in a gathering room at a hotel. Seven of the players can be identified. Joe James, first row, fourth from left; Ralph Kincaid, first row, fifth from left; Ira Simons, third row, second from right; Ernest Simons, second row, third from left; Bill Williams, second row, fourth from left; Roy Williams, drummer on left; and Bill Tiffany, first row, third from left.

This picture was taken in 1907 and when it appeared in the paper it was titled *A Bunch of Has Beens.* They are listed by age and not position in the picture. Lorenzo Parker, 91; John Horan, 88; Uncle Joe Rinear, 86; J. C. James Sr., 81; Abe Crowley, 78; C. B. Harrison, 73; Eli Judd, 73; Cyrus Proctor, 72; Joseph Savage, 69; L. K. Willett, 65; J. B. Burnett, 64; James Britton, 63; Mike Sheehan, 63; Walter Stickles, 62; James Kay, 60; John Drury, 52; and B. F. Van Patten, 52.

Fishing at Cross Lake in 1906 was good. From left to right are (first row) Ed Wells, Almond Webb, James Kay, John Drury, James Britton, and Robert McDougal; (second row) Joseph Savage, Mr. Curtis, Mr. Carman, Joseph Rinear, Harm Bryant, Walter Crowley, "Egg" Hoysradt, Cyrus Proctor, John Spafford (seated in rear), and Jerome Burnett; (third row) Abe Crowley, Joe Miller, Fred Ackerman, Joseph Huber, Frank Van Patten, Nick Schroeder, and M. Molitor.

This wonderful picture of the men of Antioch who fought in the "War of Rebellion" was probably taken in the 1890s. They were members of the Grand Army of the Republic (GAR) fraternal organization. Although their names have been lost, what they did will always be remembered. The GAR was started on April 6, 1866, in Decatur to help the veterans of the Union Army to return to normal life. By 1890, the membership had swollen to 409,489. The last member died in 1956 at the age of 109.

The Smart family farm was located at what is now the northwest corner of Route 173 and Tiffany Road. These three young, beautiful girls would all play a part in the growth of Antioch. Standing is Emma Smart (who married Ernest L. Simons of the Simon's Hotel), kneeling is Gertie Smart (who would later marry J. Ernest Brook), and in the carriage is baby Pauline (who married Howard Smith of the Smith Hotel at Channel Lake).

In 1905, Susie Morley purchased the first car in Antioch. She delighted in taking friends and family for trips around the town. One can only imagine the bravery of her passengers as they bumped along the dirt roads. Morley was far ahead of her time. She married Chase Webb on New Year's Day in 1908 in Chicago, and they had a wonderful life together.

The 1910 swimming attire is certainly glamorous. There is no worry about sunburn but actual swimming was probably difficult. These young ladies knew how to have fun. From left to right are Miss Layman, Helen Nabor, Ethel Plack, Mary Sheehan, Pattie Scheurer, Edna Plack, and "Bob" Scheurer.

These lovely ladies called themselves the "Jolly Dozen." One can only imagine how much fun they must have had posing for this picture. From left to right are Susie Morley Webb, Maud Simons Sabin, Gertie Smart Brook, Pauline Smart Simons, Edna McVey Warriner, Pearl Lux Doose, unidentified, Marion Davis, Ada Lux Overton, and Alice Emmons.

Bidding Farewell To Antioch Boys Leaving To Fight For Uncle Sam. May, 2, 1918.

Antioch has always been a huge supporter of service men and women. How true when, on a cold day in May 1918, the entire town turned out to see the "boys" off to war. In 1917, seventeen young men enlisted. When school was over in May 1918, more went. In all, Antioch sent 83 boys to battle. The town fared well, as only one son was lost to the cause. Cpl. Willard J. Mann is the only name on the war memorial as being lost in the "War to end all Wars."

This photograph is of five young men who accepted the call to arms. From left to right are Archie Maplethorpe, Joe Fernandez, John Bernard "Red" Fields, John Miller, and Andrew Cobb. Others who went are Harry Radke, Harry Cushing, Clyde Fields, John Mueller, Frank Cobb, Ray Webb, Charles Tiffany, and Melton R. Park. The bells of the churches in town rang out for them at 11:00 a.m.

Seated in the center of this rare Civil War–era photograph is Levi Simons. He joined Company F, 37th Illinois Infantry at 19 years of age. After spending more than three years in service, being wounded, catching typhoid, and traveling thousands of miles by foot and rail, he returned home. Unable to do much physical work he became the proprietor of the Simons Hotel and was a most popular gentleman in town.

This photograph from the late 1940s shows how Antioch has always honored the people who serve the country. Names are not important here as these people represent all of the citizens of the area.

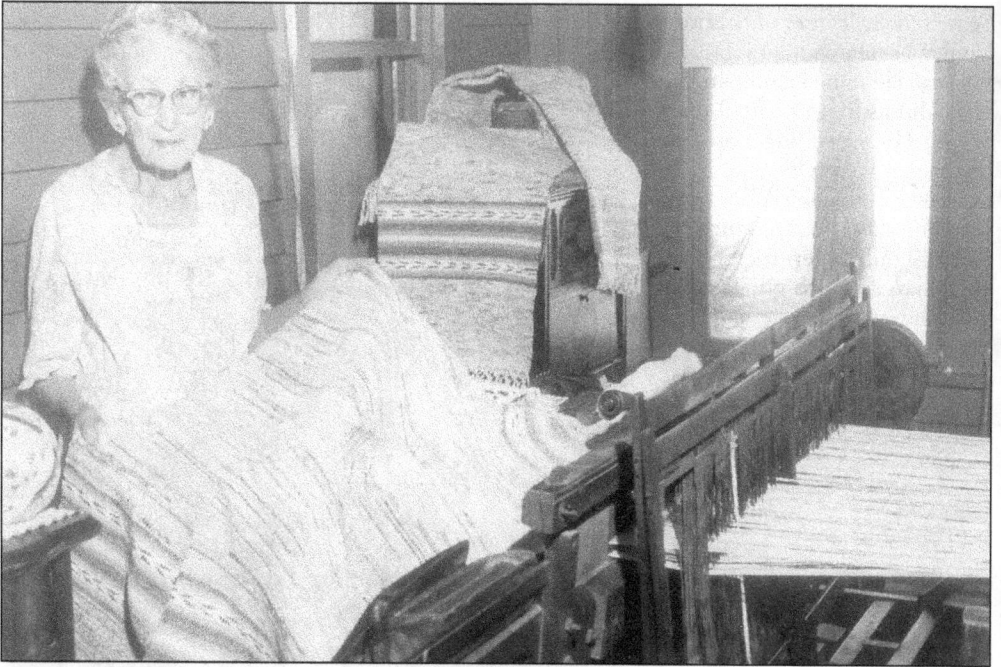

This is Lydia Proctor Horton, who was born on October 2, 1867, in a log cabin, lived all her life in the Antioch area, and was known for her woven rugs. Everyone would bring her their old clothes and rags and she would weave them into the rugs. This loom is on display at the Lakes Region Historical Society and the rug she started at age 93 is still on the loom. Aunt Lyd lived until 1961.

Taken in 1910, this photograph is of a mother and daughter. Mother Ida James Osmond is on the right and her daughter Carolyn Osmond Horan to the left. It is believed that this photograph was taken in front of John C. James's house (pictured on page 12).

The Pullen family was another of the early families to settle in Antioch. This photograph was taken in the 1890s. They are (first row) unidentified, Charles Pullen, Sarah Pullen, and David Pullen; (second row) Mary Pullen, Wayne Pullen, and Sadie Pullen. (Courtesy of Clara Drom Horton.)

Many of these young girls would have lifelong friendships and contribute to the growth of Antioch. They are, from left to right, Mildred La Plant, Vera Kincade, Gertrude Berherns, Marguerite Savage, Myrtle Haynes, Eunice ?, Julia Loma, and Margaret Neman.

These two young men, Boyd Osmond (left) and Bill Brook (right), were having a great time. They had just come from skiing on the hill by Antioch Lake and stopped to have their picture taken. The house behind them is the Nabor house. This house sits on the southwest corner of Lake Street and Hillside Avenue and is a lovely home that may soon be gone in the name of progress.

Baseball was (and still is) a passionate sport in Antioch. The Antioch Aces were together for some time and some of the players went on to play professional ball. They would play other teams in the area and were great. They are, from left to right, (first row) Jim Harvey, Jack Crandal, Louis "Doc" Koehn, and McCormick Salem; (second row) Bernie Schneider, Jack Effinger, unidentified, Bill Keulman, and Bruce Dalgaard.

In 1930, Hans von Holwede taught music at the Antioch Township High School and was very active in the community and the village. He was a favorite teacher and represents all the teachers who have taught the children since that first schoolroom in 1843, located on the second floor of the Munson Brothers store.

The board of trade was a most important place in the social life of the old Civil War veterans in Antioch. This small building sat on the corner of Lake and Spafford Streets. The lot was wooded and children would play in the area. The veterans would spend time sitting around the pot-bellied stove talking about the war or would get involved in a wild game of checkers.

This beautiful wedding photograph of Mabel Watson and Charles Richards was taken in 1898. These photographs were very common in those days but most of the people in them have not been identified. The photographer, A. E. Hatch of Burlington, Wisconsin, certainly had some beautiful props. Charles Richards put in the Farmer's Line telephone, which was separate from the Antioch Telephone Company. The two different lines could not call each other.

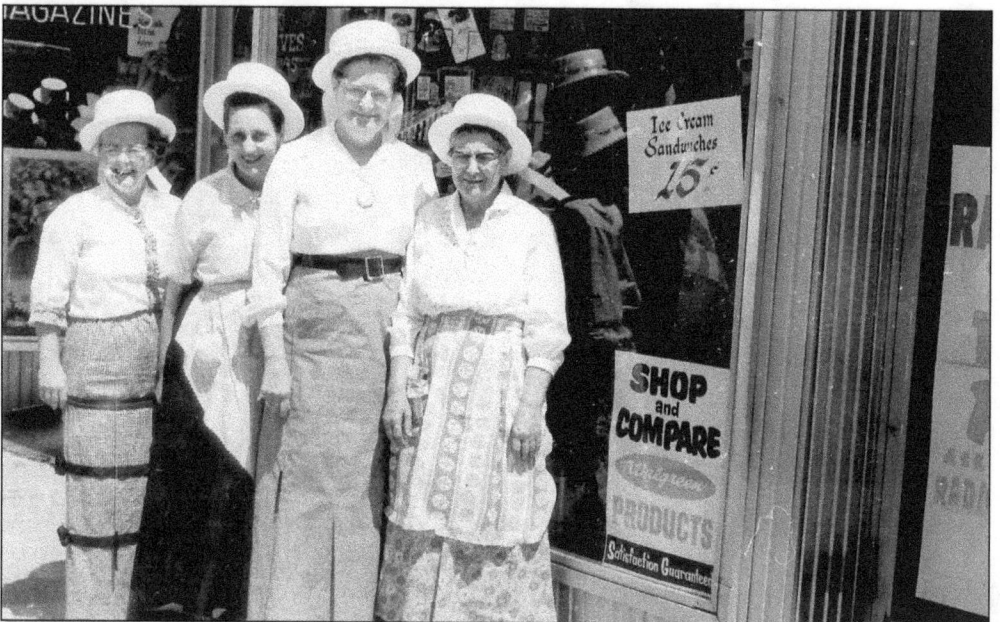

These four ladies were important to many people in Antioch. This photograph was taken in 1967 and seems strange to include in a book about early times. But Antioch is a unique town and never lost the feeling of family since the very beginning. Standing in front of Reeves Drug Store from left to right are Marge Geiger, Ruth Tarkowski, Helen Borovicka (owner/pharmacist), and Edna Drom (pharmacist).

These two gentlemen became lifelong friends because of their jobs. Neal Shultis (right) was a salesman for Steel Wedelers Wholesale Grocery, and Gus Schleicher (left) was a salesman for National Biscuit Company. They both had the same territory, so for 30 years they traveled the area together. In 1919, Shultis went into partnership with Mr. Hillebrand in the grocery business in Antioch.

These are the men who did much of the physical work in building Antioch. From left to right are Mert Haynes, Wallie Drom, Clarence Confer, and Solomon La Plant. La Plant and Haynes were brick masons and Sibley and Emmons were carpenters. On the property where the W. C. Petty School now stands, there was a brickyard where the bricks were made that built Antioch.

Taken prior to 1908, this is the final resting place for many of the early settlers in the area. This is Hillside Cemetery at Route 173 and Hillside Avenue. There are other cemeteries in the area where some of these brave people are buried. These other cemeteries include Home Oaks on Deep Lake Road near Grass Lake Road; the Grass Lake Cemetery on Grass Lake Road west of Route 59; Liberty Corners on Route 83, just south of Country Road C in Salem, Wisconsin; another one on Edwards Road, the last of Antioch; and a small one off Wilmot Road. It was not uncommon for families to have a small cemetery on the family farm. Some of those have been lost, but others have been cared for through the years. The cemeteries in the area have given the final clue to many of the early settlers in the area. Genealogists will be visiting them for years to come.

Two

THE CITY CENTER

This wonderful painting by Jacqueline Horton hangs at the Lakes Region Historical Society's School House Museum along with several others. Horton painted many, many scenes of the early Antioch area and they can be seen in many locations. Besides paintings in private collections, some can be seen in the lobby of the State Bank of the Lakes and at the Strang Funeral Home. This painting is of the southwest corner of Main Street and Lake Street. On March 20, 1891, a fire struck the entire Roger's block and destroyed the C. O. Foltz store and the smaller stores along the street. Within one year Albert Chinn had rebuilt, and the opera house was a two-story brick building 42 feet along Lake Street and 100 feet along Main Street. The opera house had a long history and part of it still stands today and houses the accounting firm of Dahl.

In 1891 shortly after the fire, construction began on the new opera house. It would be the finest around and would be able to seat hundreds of people for performances by some of the best traveling players. This crew worked hard and long to build the two-story building. All the supplies were transported by horse and buggy from the brickyard or the train station where the materials were delivered.

In 1892, G. O. Foltz opened his new store in the opera house. The store was modern and carried only the best supplies. On December 30, 1903, the Iroquois Theater in Chicago burned and 600 people perished. Foltz was devastated as his wife and two daughters were victims. That fire came only a month after another large fire had destroyed a large portion of the east side of Main Street.

By late in the second decade of the 20th century the stores on the Lake Street side of the opera house had many different tenants. This picture shows a restaurant located where the Foltz store had been. This is before 1920, as that was the year that Main Street was finally paved. No longer would the road have to be watered down to cut the dust during the dry summer months.

In October 1926, the First National Bank opened its doors for business. After extensive remodeling of the old opera house, the building looked like it does today. Charles K. Anderson was president, Robert C. Abt was a vice president, William A. Rosing was a vice president, and S. Boyer Nelson was cashier. Notice though that Lake Street still has not been paved.

This street scene is looking north on Main Street. The ever-present church steeple of the Methodist church has been a landmark since 1901. The date of this photograph is between 1915 and 1920, as in 1914 the village government decided to replace the plank sidewalks with cement and the street was not paved until 1920. (Courtesy of Thomas and Catherine [Bogan] Middlebrook.)

Note the "bus" just left of the center in front of the Williams Brothers building. This horse-drawn carriage was perhaps in from one of the resorts. This is also a rare photograph where the horses and cars are sharing the road. It did not take long for the horses to disappear from the streets of Antioch once the automobile became prevalent. (Courtesy of Thomas and Catherine [Bogan] Middlebrook.)

This picture, looking south, shows the west side of Main Street from the late 1920s. The Williams Brothers department store is in the center with the King's Drug Store just to the north. King's Drug Store had been in this same location since before 1900. When a fire damaged the building in 1950, King's had to find a new home.

World War II brought a boom to Antioch. When the young men and women returned they needed housing and jobs. This east side shot looks the same as today except that there are different shops in every store. Diagonal parking changed to parallel parking in the early 1950s when the state enacted a new law on how wide state highways had to be. Main Street is now State Route 83, originally called the Mukwonago Indian Trail. (Courtesy of Thomas and Catherine [Bogan] Middlebrook.)

This is a picture of the west side of Main Street before all these buildings were replaced with brick. The building to the far right and partially obscured by the tree is Williams Brothers. The little boy sitting in front of the shoe store is Robert Brogan. Calugi's Ice Cream store with its choice California fruits and fine candies would have been a must stop on any trip to town.

Joseph C. James was born in England in 1827. He came to the Antioch area in the 1840s and was listed in the 1860 census as a farmer. This building stood just west of the old gas station at Main Street and Orchard Street. His son Joseph C. James Jr. was in business with him and continued into the 1920s as an insurance and real estate company.

The Antioch Milling Company was at the southeast corner of Main and Depot Streets. It incorporated in 1919 but had been in business for several years before that. In 1942, it set new production records for the war effort in the processing of eggs, milk, and pigs from local farmers. The building stood and was in operation until June 1962, when it was razed for a new parking lot for Pittman Pontiac. The entire corner is now empty and would be a lovely site for a village park.

The Antioch Lumber and Coal Company boasted, in a 1923 advertisement, that it was the largest lumberyard in Lake County outside of Waukegan. It was at the corner of Depot Street and Corona Street. The street originally got its name from the factory that made the Corona fountain pens. The company provided coal to many of the year-around homes for heat during the winter months.

This very early picture shows how the town looked around 1906. There are a few cars in town and the Ford Garage, but there are no electric lines. Since Susie Morley owned the first car in Antioch in 1905 and electric lines began to be erected in 1907, then the only conclusion is that this has to be 1906.

On the left is a high-back Nash Rambler that carried a band. During the first decade of the 1900s this parade of Antioch merchants went around to the surrounding areas advertising Antioch as a great place to trade. The idea must have gotten results as business in Antioch boomed over the next few years. The William Keulman Jewelry Store is in the frame building on the right. The photograph is looking north.

The Union Block Building was built in 1903 after a fire destroyed the east side of Main Street. Here the Van Patten Saloon can be seen on the left, Osmond Furniture is in the center, and A. N. Tiffany and Company is on the right.

This photograph was taken from the top of the village's stand pipe (110 feet) and is from around 1910. The large building in the center of the picture is Williams Brothers store. The barns behind the buildings were for the horses and carriages for the respective business. Note the gardens where now a parking lot lies. The view is looking southeast and is magnificent.

In 1898, H. A. Radke purchased the barber shop and goodwill of Will Hodge. He started a family business that lasted almost 100 years. Standing in front of the shop is H. A. on the left and son Harry on the right. The location never changed and was handed down from father to son for five generations.

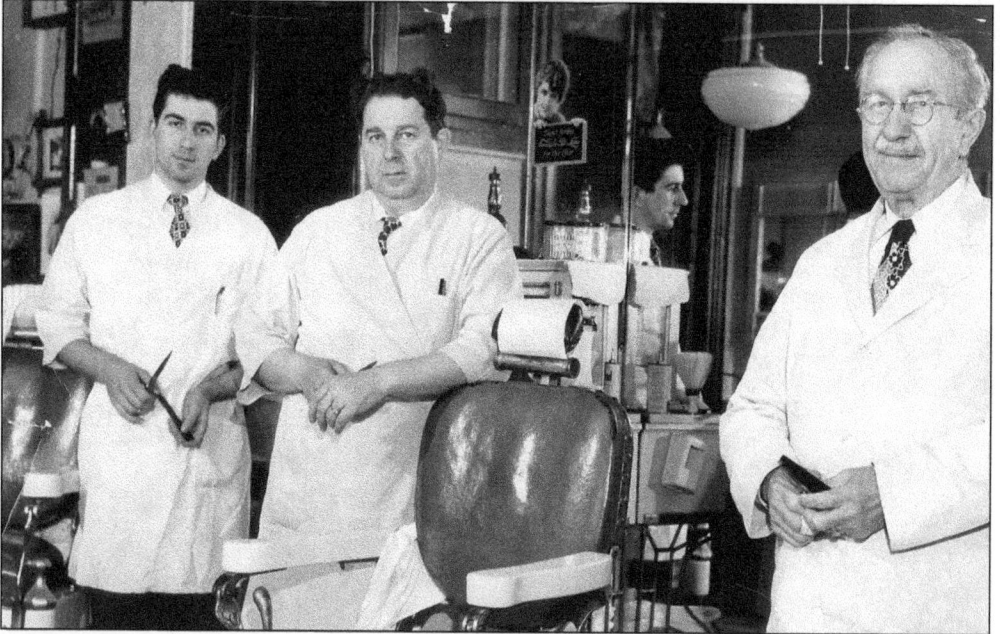

In 1951, the family posed for this picture. From left to right are Dick, Cap, and Herman Radke. The generations were H. A., Harry, Herman, Cap, and Dick. Imagine the generations of families that went to that barber shop and the stories that were told. The location, 912 Main Street, now houses Hair Designs Unlimited.

George "Dutch" Golwitzer also had a barber shop at what is now 900 Main Street. This building was replaced by a brick building sometime before 1914 when the cement sidewalks were put in. From left to right are Tom Burnett, unidentified, and George Golwitzer.

Golwitzer's Barber Shop was a popular place to go in the very early 1900s. Not only did the children love to go there for haircuts, because Dutch would give them a candy bar after a cut, but there were also two bowling lanes upstairs. When Dutch was ready to retire in 1927, Mr. Hennings opened a full recreation parlor in the location.

In 1909 a group of revelers who called themselves the Waukegan Day Advertising Committee, made a tour of Lake County ending up in Antioch in the late afternoon. They were advertising a ball game to be held between the Chicago White Sox and the Waukegan team. Their numbers had dwindled during the day and when they finally arrived in Antioch there were only a few cars left.

When it snowed the only way to get around was by horse and sleigh. No car would have made it through. This sleigh was carrying milk cans and was probably heading toward the feed mill at the end of the street. Or perhaps they were trying to get to the train station to get the product to market. Only those who absolutely needed to go out would brave the wrath of Mother Nature.

In the very early days the only way to get meat for dinner was to go out and hunt it. As farms became established domestic meat became available. Farmers would have chickens, pigs, and cows. The dairy industry was good because of the rich vegetation. The Antioch Meat Market opened to provide fresh meat for the growing population. Located on Main Street in the 900 block it was next to Overton Drug Store, which would later become King's.

This is the interior of the Whitcher and Shotliff Meat Market (also named the Antioch Meat Market) around 1900. The picture speaks for itself. This was not a place that the ladies would go. Pictured from left to right are Fred Shotliff, Charles Powles, and two unidentified customers.

Since Charles Powles (second from left) was working at the Antioch Meat Market, as seen in the previous photograph, it is assumed that he opened his own shop, as there continued to be a meat market at the Shotliff location. The current address of this building is 390 Lake Street. The gentleman standing on the left is Ernest Brook, the banker from next door at 388 Lake Street. The identity of the two young ladies is unknown.

After the Bank of Antioch moved to a new location on Main Street and changed its name to Brook Bank, Powles moved his meat market into the larger building next door. An old-timer remembered that if a child went with their parents into the meat market, Powles would give the child a hot dog. In this photograph his old store is still empty waiting for its next tenant. At the far end of the building was the Walters Photographic Studio.

Powles (left) and his son Frank (right) pose inside their store at 388 Lake Street around 1920. This is a shop where the ladies could feel comfortable shopping. With the variety of items, the ladies could get many other products to make the meat tastier. The tiny tile floor is still under the carpeting in that building. An interesting note is how the authors had a small retail store in the 1990s in this building and found and cleaned the floor under the linoleum.

In the early days there were several meat markets in the community. There were also so many fires that most of the original buildings from the late 1800s do not exist anymore. Such is true for this one at 510 Main Street. It burned to the ground in March 1930 with a loss of over $10,000. It was too far from the water source and could not be saved. Today another meat market stands in its place next to the railroad tracks—Antioch Packing House.

Edward Brook of Burlington, Wisconsin, opened the Bank of Antioch in 1894. This was the beginning of the long history of today's State Bank of the Lakes. In March 1901, Chinn block and the Bank of Antioch burned in an overnight fire. Due to the lack of any fire protection, the buildings were a smoldering ruin. It was believed that the fire started in the storage room of the Somerville Bakery. This building was a two-story brick building that had been built over the ruins of the original frame building that had burned in the 1891 fire. In 1903, Edward Brook and Charles Thorn rebuilt the Chinn block. Thorn occupied the west end while the Bank of Antioch had the east end. In 1924, the Bank of Antioch purchased the property on Main Street known as the Great Front Store. In 1926, after some remodeling, the newly named Brook Bank opened a new, modern facility.

The State Bank of Antioch opened in February 1903 in the Somerville Building. The bank had been organized under the laws of the State of Illinois with E. B. Williams, G. O. Paddock, W. S. Westlake, R. L. Strang, and Joseph Turner as directors. Eventually the two banks would merge with the Brook family in control. The upper floor of this building was used by the Masons and Odd Fellows and was built of Bedford, Indiana, stone and bricks.

This photograph is of the interior of the State Bank of Antioch at its location at 934 Main Street. The beautiful balcony with its east facing window captured the morning sunlight that lit up the marble used throughout. The door to the right of the picture was a modern ladies' room. The elegance of the 1920s is timeless.

(BUDS)

Morley's Saloon was perhaps one of the most popular establishments in town. It was a place where the men in town could meet and talk and relax. Of course in the early days, ladies were not allowed inside. Morley's eventually became Bud's Tap well into the mid-1900s. In the early 1960s, the building was condemned and torn down. It is a lovely park today on the west side of Main Street near the middle of town.

GAUGER BROS.

In 1906, the Gauger Brothers store was a wonderful place to shop. The ladies could choose anything from apples to lace curtains and many other types of finery. The owners decided in early 1913 to close. Competition was a fact even then. From left to right are an unidentified woman and baby, Kittie Clark, Alex Gauger, Frank Stickler, Arthur Herman, Margaret Pullen, Bertha and Nellie Gauger (sisters of Alex), and James Wilton.

48

William Keulman opened his store in the very early 1900s. This photograph was taken in 1907 in front of the first store with his children Olive Irene and William George. He not only offered fine jewelry but was also an optician and provided eye glasses to his customers. The store continued to grow but never left its original location at 913 Main Street.

Right in the center of the photograph one can see the William Keulman Jewelry Store. This was one of the areas that was destroyed by fire and rebuilt with brick. The Keulman store stayed in business for many long years—well into the second half of the 1900s. The Keulman family was very involved in community activities.

This building was built prior to 1843 and was used by the Munson brothers. The second floor was the first school. It housed the very first general store in Antioch in the 1850s. It became Emmons Drugs, then J. E. Hill Drugs, and then Swan Drugs. It would be Overton Drugs before Frank King bought the business.

After the passing of Bert Overton, Mrs. Overton took on Frank King to be the pharmacist in the store. In 1914, King purchased the business from Mrs. Overton. This photograph is from 1912 and still shows the horse tie-ups in front of the shops along Main Street. It also shows that the Antioch Meat Market is now under the ownership of Rolla A. Shultis.

In 1871, the wooden structure known as the King building was purchased by Levi Simons. By 1924, the old landmark was beyond repair and was destroyed and rebuilt. The new building was built strong and, except for an internal fire in the 1950s, is still standing next to the Williams Brothers building. (Courtesy of Thomas and Catherine [Bogan] Middlebrook.)

During the time period that the King building was being redone, King's Drug Store had to have a place to do business. It moved south on Main Street next to the new State Bank of Antioch. When the new building was ready the store moved back and remained there until it moved to 400 Lake Street in December 1963. It eventually moved to 939 Main Street before closing its doors in the 1980s.

Sidney "Daddy" Reeves was considered the "dean of businessmen" for the first half of the 1900s. In 1919, he moved to Antioch to be the relief pharmacist for the Richards' Drug Store. He purchased the business and made Antioch his home. In February 1942, the Borovickas purchased the drug store and began a Walgreens agency. Reeves Drug Store remained one of the most recognized landmarks in Antioch until the 1970s.

This is the interior of Reeves with a customer and employees. From left to right are two unidentified workers, a young Ed Strang, unidentified, Sidney Reeves, Ruth Cribb Eliott, Edna Drom, and owner Helen Borovicka. The memories of the wonderful sodas and ice-cream sundaes are still fresh. How about a banana split? Or a cherry fizz?

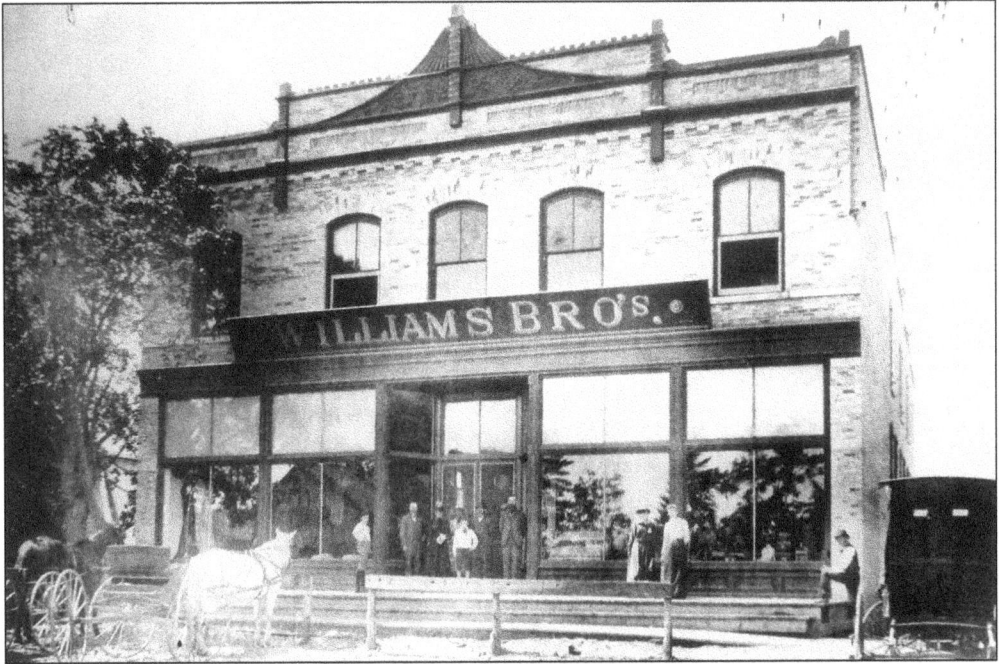

The Willams Brothers store was one of the finest built in Antioch in 1890–1891. Mr. Cashmore, the town brick maker, was said to have distinguished himself by making the kiln that produced the most excellent bricks. The store was finished in late 1890, and on New Year's Day, 1891, the gas was turned on. The new lights gave the store a most metropolitan air.

The interior of the store shows how versatile the selections were. Who would need to go anywhere else? On the floor are several large watermelons probably from a local farm. On the left was the area that the ladies would spend much time looking at the newest fabrics. On the top shelf on the right are beautiful lamps that would enhance any home.

With the rapid growth of the automobile industry, the gas station industry had to grow faster. Stations began to pop up all over town. One of the earliest was Kaye's Service Station located at the southeast corner of Main Street and Park Avenue. At this time in the early 1920s, the station had Red Crown gasoline and Racine Multi-Mile cord tires. This station would later become Red Murrie's Standard Station.

On the other corner of Main Street and Park Avenue (now a parking lot) was Bert's Sinclair Station. This photograph is from about 1930. Bert also had aircraft fuel available as there were a couple of small airstrips in the area. Earlier the Ford Garage had carried Texaco Gas. These are only two of the many, many stations in the area.

The *Antioch News* played one of the most important parts in the growth of Antioch. Founded in August 1886 by J. J. Burke, it is responsible for much of the history that has been saved for today. The original building burned in the fire of 1891, but Burke had the paper back in print before the ashes were cold.

Saturday evening was the time of the week that people could relax and enjoy friends. One old-timer remembered when he was a kid, his dad would take the car to town and find a choice parking spot. Dad would then walk home, the family would have dinner and then all walk to town where the car was parked. They would sit and converse with others who had done the same.

The ice-cutting industry was huge in the late 1890s into the 1930s. Practically every lake in the area had at least one icehouse on its shore. As the water froze in the winter, men would brave the cold weather and cut ice. It would be stored in icehouses and shipped via rail to the city during the summer months. Once the electric refrigerator became popular, the ice industry was no longer needed. The Esch Brothers and Ray Ice House was on Loon Lake where Lyn Barthel was superintendent for seven years.

From left to right these workers are Frank Dempsere, Lyn Barthel, and Joe Greberry. Barthel invented the loading machine that he is operating. It was used for moving the ice in and out of the ice house and onto the wagons that moved the blocks to the trains for shipment to the city. The ice industry employed a great number of men during the winter months of the late 1800s into the 1930s.

This beautiful truck from about 1920 was made by the White Motor Company, which was a spin off of the White Sewing Machine Company that started in 1876. The sons of Thomas White made steam powered automobiles from 1901 until 1918 and then turned their attention to trucks only. The Antioch Lumber and Coal Company got many years of great service from this truck.

Since this entire area was excellent for dairy farming, there were several dairies in the area. Scott's Dairy off North Avenue was owned by the longtime police chief Walter Scott, known around town as Scottie. The Golden Glo Guernsey Dairy made home deliveries for many years. The Willowdale Dairy had a large fire on September 21, 1959, but deliveries were not interrupted.

There is one important business that everyone eventually needs. In 1898, George E. Strang purchased a funeral and furniture business in Grayslake. His son Lee had followed in his father's footsteps and learned the carpenter trade. When the White funeral home came up for sale in Antioch after 1911, George purchased it. Leland Strang attended the College of Embalming in Chicago and received his Illinois and Wisconsin embalmer's licenses in July 1919. The business was located at 896 Main Street. In 1933, Leland purchased the Charles Thorn farmhouse at 1055 Main Street and moved there. He added an addition in 1941. This beautiful 1917 Model Reo rear-loading hearse was purchased in March 1920. Standing in front are Leland on the left and George E. on the right. Strang Funeral Home continued in the family with Ed Strang taking control in 1950. Ed retired in 1976 and sold the business to Dan Dugenske, who is still the owner today.

Three

RELIGION AND EDUCATION

Antioch School.

M. E. Church, Antioch Ill.

Two of the most identifiable landmarks in Antioch are the Methodist church and the old schoolhouse. Anyone driving north on Route 83 will immediately recognize the steeple of the church. It has stood for over 100 years and is a sign for many that they are home. The schoolhouse stands for the very basic right of all children to get a good education. The old school still has a hand in the teaching of children as many classes, Boy Scout and Girl Scout troops, and others tour the museum on a regular basis. The excitement of these children is evident when they bring their parents back to show them the great history.

The first church in Antioch was the Disciples of Christ Church. Built in 1863, the simple frame, white building served the congregation for many, many years. In 2000, the Lakes Region Historical Society received a bequeath from Dolly Spiering, which allowed the group to purchase the building to save it from demolition. The society decided to renovate the building to its original look and it is now a museum at 977 Main Street.

The congregation of St. Ignatius Episcopal Church had been renting the old church above and looking for a suitable place to build a new church. In 1916, they decided to purchase the church and renovate it. Although the building was more than 50 years old, it was in excellent shape and the people of St. Ignatius just added their needs to it. The original foundation from 1863 can still be seen today. The World War I Fort Sheidan barrack was added in 1926 to provide more space.

The first Church of Christ Scientist, although not having a building to call home, started meeting in member's homes in 1914. By 1917, the number had grown and services were held in various public building such as the Majestic Theater, Odd Fellows hall, and the Chinn Hall until 1928. In 1923, the society became a recognized society of the mother church, the First Church of Christ Scientist, in Boston, Massachusetts. In 1928, a generous merchant, whose wife had a healing in Christian Science, erected a permanent building for their use. That location was at 955 Victoria Street. The building pictured was erected in 1966 and the congregation moved to the church on the hill. This simple Colonial-style church overlooks Antioch Lake from its home at the corner of Route 173 and Harden Street. Due to the times, the small group held the last service on Sunday, April 11, 2004. The building was sold.

The Catholic Church built this small white frame building in 1896 on Victoria Street. At first services could only be held when a priest would come out from the city. St. Peter's Parish was actually started in 1900 by Fr. M. Bruton. The beautiful bell in front of the church was donated by Dr. Charles Venn in 1912.

The cornerstone for the new Catholic church was laid on July 1, 1929, with an impressive ceremony led by Bishop Sheil. The completed church was dedicated on August 10, 1930. Cardinal Mundelein conducted the rites. (Courtesy of the Village of Antioch.)

In its 77 years, this sanctuary has seen thousands of weddings, baptisms, and funerals as well as the several services each week. The number of people who have been touched by its beauty will never be fully known and the number of lives changed is known only to God. (Courtesy of Thomas and Catherine [Bogan] Middlebrook.)

This aerial shot of the area is indeed impressive. The new Catholic Complex, the Hillside Cemetery, and Lake Antioch provide a stunning look at the area in the 1930s. The land on which the church is built was donated by Bernard F. Nabor from his farmland.

This white frame building was also built in 1863 on the location that is now the parking lot for the United Methodist Church. The Baptists built the church, but in 1879, the Methodist Episcopal Church began meeting there. The wooden structure served the congregation until the current building was erected in 1901.

This good looking group of people is the congregation of the Methodist Episcopal church around 1893. The pastor at that time was Clarence Abel. It is so good to see so many smiles as it is very uncommon to see in these older pictures. Obviously these people had a peace of mind and a strong faith in the Lord. The names of the members are available at the Lakes Region Historical Society.

A very large version of this photograph hangs in the Lakes Region Historical Society Meeting House Museum at 977 Main Street. The rectory of the Methodist Episcopal church sits in the middle with the Sequoit Creek running through. The cows are content and blissfully unaware of the activity around them as they graze on the property that is now a gas station.

Because the Antioch High School had not yet been built (it would be built in 1915), the high school students met in one of the rooms at the schoolhouse at Depot Street and Main Street. For the seven students that passed all graduation requirements, the sanctuary of the Methodist Episcopal church served as a backdrop for the ceremony.

In the winter of 1842–1843, school became available for the children. The first class was held in an upper, unfinished room in the general store owned by F. F. Munson. Welcome Jilson taught these first classes. The school moved around the town, space permitting, until a permanent location was built in 1873. This frame building was only one room and heated by a large pot-bellied stove.

The children would sit on long, hard benches and had to provide their own slates and books. No wonder they are all frowning. The private facilities stood outside, and there was no running water. The children would get drinks from the village pump that stood in the road. The original pump is on display at the Lakes Region Historical Society's School House Museum.

In 1892, this brick, five-room schoolhouse was erected. This east side view shows the fire escape from the second floor. The large windows let in lots of light and the children could now be schooled in smaller classes. New teachers were hired and education became even more important in the lives of children.

The formal dedication of the new school was in November 1928. What a beautiful, modern building, and in 1941 the first kindergarten class in the Chain O' Lakes region was held here. The 1892 building stands just to the outside on the left of the picture. The large porch area was a favorite place to play. The authors spent their grade-school years, kindergarten through eighth grades, in this building.

Even with the new building right next to them, these third graders still had class in the 1892 building. This room is the first-floor south room and today has many wonderful displays about the early days of Antioch. The wooden floor was refinished in the 1980s but is still the original floor.

The eighth-grade class of 1929 had several notable students. The teacher was W. C. Petty, who would later become the superintendent of schools in Lake County. They are, from left to right, (first row) Wilma Musch, Berneice Risch, Marion Smith, Hazel Hawkins, Marjorie Singer, Betty Warriner, and June Allner; (second row) Gwendolyn Girard, Lillian Vykruta, Lee Roy, Bill Keulman, Evelyn Hennings, Wilbur Whitmire, Sherman Ferris, Bill Brook, Harold Nelson, Donald Snyder, and Williams Water; (third row) Homer Fawcett, Laurel Van Patten, Eileen Osmond, Estelle Luhas, Dan Williams, Carl Hattendorf, Joe Pachay, Dorothy Musch, Stub Murrie, Margaret Sullivan, and W. C. Petty.

Channel Lake School was on Lake Street, which is several miles west of town, off Route 173. The school eventually merged with district No. 34 as did many other smaller schools such as Johnson, Bean Hill, Grubb, Oakland, and Hickory. This is a picture of the lower grades in 1948–1949. The names of these adorable children are being withheld as many of them are still walking the streets of Antioch.

Although not a historic school, St. Peter's School has played an important role since it was built in 1949. It helped to relieve the ever growing burden on the public schools as well as giving the children of the Catholic Church a religion-based education. These four classrooms and gym were added after 1960. (Courtesy of the Village of Antioch.)

This group of students attended Emmons School south of town in the 1921–1922 school year. From left to right are (first row) Raymond Burnette, Charles Ferris, Anna Edlmann, Dorothy Ferris, Herman Edlmann, Vera Bown, Helen Burnette, Anna Zitko, William Potter, Helen Frown, Rabena Gray, and Bobbie Squibbs; (second row) John Litko, Morris Bown, Marguerite Kufalk, Olive Message, Mildred Robinson, Othelia Cook, Anna Blanchard, Ardis Toft, Leonard Armstrong, and Carl Frown; (third row) Clarence Kufalk, Robert Runyard, Wilma Proffett, Susan Zitko, teacher Ida Runyard Kufalk, Helen Blanchard, Eleanor Cobb, and Herbert Brown.

Although Emmons School is close to Antioch, only a couple of miles south on Route 83, it has maintained its independence. In 1955, there were talks between the school boards of Emmons and district No. 34 but a merge never materialized. Today the school maintains a fully rounded school serving children from kindergarten to eighth grade with a very active parent group. (Courtesy of the Village of Antioch.)

Yes, there was an Oakland School long before the present one. The little white frame building stood on the northwest corner of Grass Lake Road and Deep Lake Road. Very similar to all the other one-room schools built in the 1890s and early 1900s, it educated mostly farm families from the surrounding area.

In 1922, the little one-room building was replaced by a modern building right next to it. The school had several rooms and the children could be separated by grade. Then in 1957, the school district put a referendum on the ballot and it passed 2 to 1 in favor of building a new school at the Oakland site. That school was built with expansion in mind, and as enrollment grew, rooms were finished to accommodate the students.

High School,
Antioch, Ill.

3. Brooks Photo

The cornerstone for the high school was laid in 1915. That stone is now on display at the School House Museum outside the entrance door (when the current addition was added, that stone was removed). This photograph was taken after the first of many additions had been added. Enrollment continued to grow with the community and the school needed to keep up.

HIGH SCHOOL. ANTIOCH, ILL. 86-R

More additions expanded the opportunities for the students. Thousands of people have walked through these halls. Football teams, band and choir, and dozens of other activities rounded out an education for the future. This photograph shows the old school section that had to come down during the 1990s to make room for newer facilities.

Four

THOSE WHO SERVE

The village government has always been the ongoing force to keep Antioch growing. This photograph is of Mayor George Bartlett, mayor from May 1929 through October 1949. Bartlett died while in office and a pro tem was appointed to fill out his term. He is standing next to an artillery piece received from the federal government in 1935. This has since been replaced with a tank. Along with the village officers, it takes several other service agencies to complete the community. Citizens today need postal service, library services, fire protection, a rescue squad, clean water, and dozens of other things that the early settlers did not have. Here is a small representation of the brave souls that provided the community with commitment.

THE VILLAGE PARK AND PUMPING STATION, ANTIOCH, ILL.

The village park has been a meeting place for several decades. It may be small but the meaning is very intense. The cement platform that the artillery sits upon was actually the base for the very first stand pipe to provide water to the community in 1907. In current times, during the month of December, children can visit Santa at his castle that magically appears at Thanksgiving.

This building, built in the early 1900s, was used as the village hall and fire station. It is at 875 Main Street. As other growth continued, it eventually became the police station. The front facade has changed slightly but the original structure remained the same. It was in use until the new village building across the street was ready and then put up for sale in 1969.

Police chief Walter Scott, known to many as Scottie, used his own car until the village board finally approved the purchase of a squad car in 1951. His faithful companion, whose name is lost, went with him whenever possible. Scottie was also the owner of Scott's Dairy on North Avenue. He also served the community in many other ways as a village trustee, a fireman, and a member of the rescue squad. He served over 16 years as chief.

In August 1955, Bob Lindblad, owner of E and L Pontiac Incorporated Agency (and father of the authors), presented the auxiliary police their own squad car. Accepting the keys from Bob are Ray Toft, who would later become mayor, and Art Meyer, a businessman in town. E and L Pontiac would later become Pittman Pontiac.

In 1907 the decisions was made that the village needed a stand pipe to supply water for the village and fire protection. The village purchased a lot owned by Mary Williams, which was behind the Simons Hotel. The lot cost $300. Solomon La Plant's crew put the tower up without the modern methods of today. The stand pipe was 110 feet high and took over 20,000 bricks to complete. It cost a total of $7,163 to build. When the stand pipe was replaced in 1935, the base was not removed. It would later become the base of the war memorial at the southwest corner of Orchard and Toft Streets. Prior to this time, water was available from a village pump at the corner of Depot Street and Main Street near the school. When the stand pipe went up the pump was covered over. Look closely at the very right of the photograph to see where the Methodist church steeple pops up.

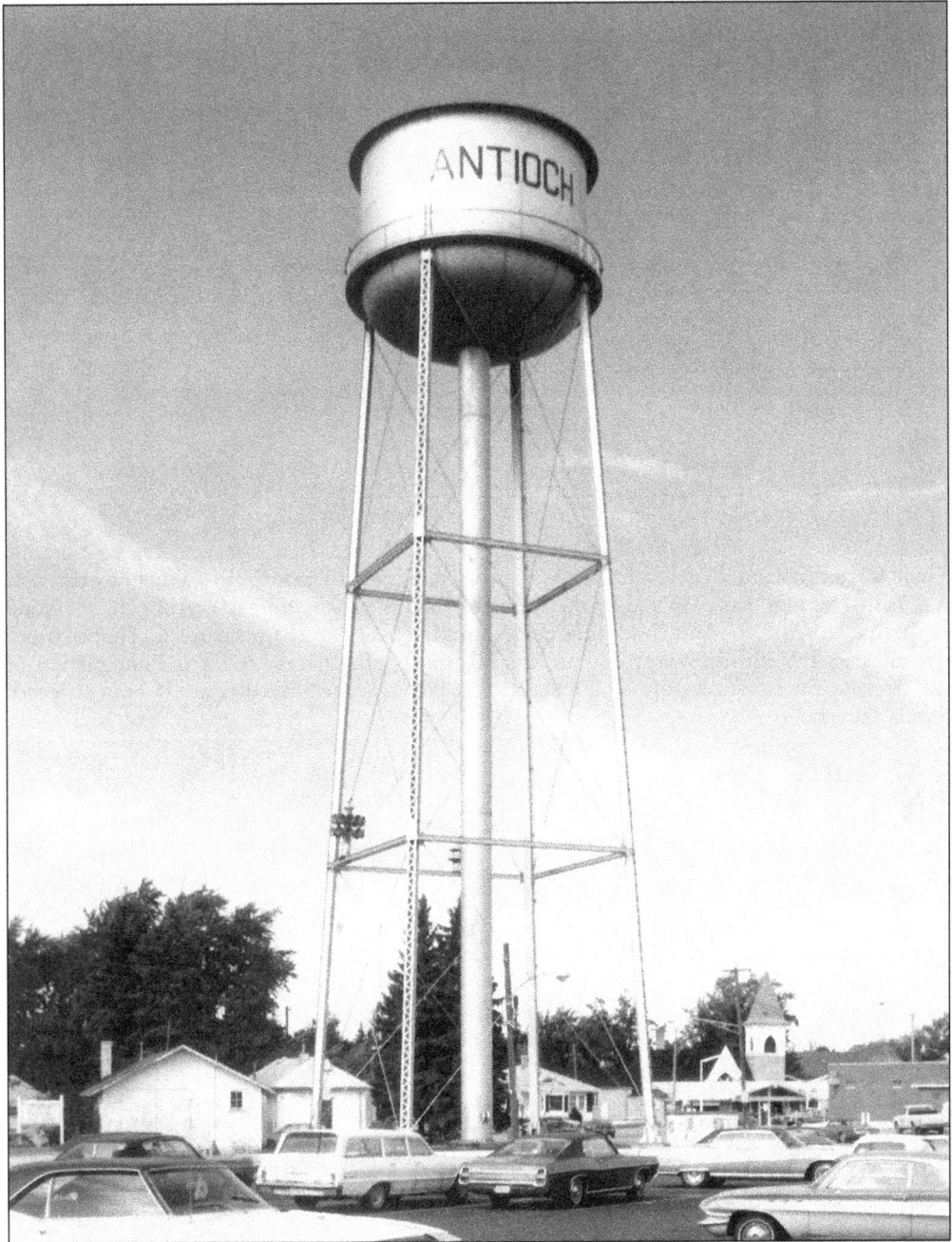

The village government decided in 1935 that the old tower needed replacement. It could not keep up with the demand of the village. The village officials applied for a federal grant and received $5,000 toward the new tower. The total cost would come to $10,140.50. The old stand pipe held 40,000 gallons of water while the new one would hold 120,000 gallons. Harold "Red" Rowling worked on the new tower that was built by Chicago Bridge and Iron. It becomes apparent how much larger this tower was by comparing the Methodist Church Steeple in the two pictures. This tower is slated to come down in the very near future. It served the community well for over 72 years.

There was excitement all through the town as the word came that the train was coming through Antioch. The year was 1885 and by the spring of 1886 the track came into Antioch. Everyone knew that this was the best thing that could have happened to the small town. That summer the rail cars ran through everyday carrying all the supplies necessary for the completion of the track to the north. It only took a short time before scenes like this would be seen every Sunday afternoon.

The taxis are waiting for the Saturday afternoon train. Many of the larger resorts would have their own carriage and others would depend on the various public conveyances. Imagine getting tied up in this traffic jam. After a short ride to the town hotel or a bumpy one out to a resort the evening was waiting with good food and dance.

This original station built in 1886 needed a new coat of paint in 1899. It actually was located on the east side of the tracks south of Depot Street. This train was headed north. The trains passing through not only carried passengers but freight as well. Local merchants would order supplies from the city and they would be shipped out by train.

This must have been a very warm summer day as the gentlemen have all removed their jackets. There do not appear to be any ladies in this group. Perhaps they all rode together in the other end of the train. It took between one and two hours to make it out here. That was a long time to bump along the tracks and try to stay looking fresh. (Courtesy of Thomas and Catherine [Bogan] Middlebrook.)

The Wisconsin Central Railway had several stops along the way. Antioch was not the only destination. Some of the other stops were Gray's Lake (name taken from a ticket), Lake Villa, Silver Lake (Wisconsin), Burlington, Mukwonago, Waukesha, Fond du Lac, Oshkosh, Waupaca, Ashland, and Duluth, Minnesota.

A new depot was built in 1922 on the opposite side of the tracks. It also moved to the other side of Depot Street (very near the present station). The old steam engine is belching smoke as the fog starts to settle in. (Courtesy of Thomas and Catherine [Bogan] Middlebrook.)

Meeting the Afternoon Train, Antioch, Ill.   8158-r

By the late 1920s the crowds were not as thick, as many people had their own cars. The trip out to the lakes was made easier when they drove themselves. The independent nature of Americans came through as more and more people bought their own transportation. And many of them even moved out from the city to make Antioch a permanent home. (Courtesy of Thomas and Catherine [Bogan] Middlebrook.)

As the days of the trains began to wane because of better roads and faster cars, passenger service came to an end. Trains would still follow the tracks past the old station, but they never stopped. They carried freight to the large cities of the Midwest. The old station sat quietly waiting and watching. Vandals struck, and in August 1976, the building crumbled in a fire. A few months later the Soo Line obtained a permit and the final death came to the old building. But by the 1990s, a new era began and a new station was built to provide for the new commuter line.

This beautiful little house, the home to the Edgar B. Williams family, was built in 1885. Along the way, the Edgar B. Williams Homestead became the property of William E. Schroeder. According to the marriage index, Williams's daughter married a Schroeder. In 1950, he deeded the property to the Antioch Township Library. An addition was added and the library finally had a permanent home.

The remodeled home served as the area library for many years. In 1966, a new library was proposed by the board. It was a bittersweet thing for librarian Betty Lu Williams as this had been her ancestral home. When the new building was ready in 1970, the home was demolished. The picture is all that is left to remember the good times in the little library.

Leroy D. Gage, one of the first settlers in the area, was the first postmaster. An official post office was established in December 1845. Prior to that, mail was picked up at Brass Ball Tavern where people would take turns going for it. Later they would get the mail from Wadsworth. Mail was a little uncertain in those days. This picture is of Burt Hoyt, around 1914.

The post office was not to have a permanent home until 1961. Look to the right edge of the photograph and one will see a home of the post office. In the 1890s it had space in Williams Brothers. It spent time in Gambles, First National Bank, a store front at 917 Main Street, and a store front at Lake Street and Victoria Street. Finally in 1961, a new building was erected at the Orchard Street location. That location is still in use as well as the newer facility near there.

This is the same building as the bottom image on page 74. The building is 22 feet wide and 60 feet long. The front 36 feet is for the fire department while the back room housed the village offices. It was built of brick because of the many fires that had taken place in the village and was only a block away from the stand pipe.

For many years the *Antioch News* had advocated that someone do something about the inadequate fire protection in the village. In 1890, Burlington was selling this hand pumper, and the *Antioch News* was adamant about some of the village businessmen finding a way to purchase it. The editor finally got his wish when the pumper was brought into town.

These volunteer firemen are working with the hand pumper. The large building in the background is the opera house. They are, from left to right, unidentified, Bill Davis, John Horan, unidentified, unidentified, and Clete Van Patten. There were still many wooden structures in the town and spending time with the pumper to learn all about it was no different in that time than now.

The fire bell was first placed next to the stand pipe and pumping station. At this location, it was behind many of the stores, and when it rang only a few people could hear it. It was moved more than once, but a good location could not be found where everyone could hear it ringing. There had been major fires in 1891, 1901, and 1903 within the few blocks of town.

This modern 1921 Stoughton fire truck, made by Stoughton Wagon Works in Stoughton, Wisconsin, became fire truck No. 1 when purchased in 1923. The village paid $5,700 for it. Now the fire department had some of the best equipment available.

When a new truck was purchased (next page) the old No. 1 was sold to Rockland. Then in 1954, it was up for sale as an antique and George Borovicka, the owner of Reeves Drug Store, bought it and brought it home. Clarence Shultis drove old No. 1 in parades. It is still around and the proud possession of the Antioch Fire Department.

The new truck was also purchased from Stoughton Wagon Works in about 1931. Here it is seen sitting in front of the new grade school that was dedicated in 1928. This larger truck had more hose and power.

The pride of the Antioch Volunteer Fire Department was the truck. Next to the truck is one of the Antioch police officers on a super motorbike. Note in the center of the photograph the small sign on the building—Public Library. That was just one of the many homes it had. The Crystal Theatre next door was playing the latest movie.

FIREMEN'S BOOSTER PARADE
ANTIOCH ILL.

MYERS
850

Around 1910, the volunteers of the fire department started having a picnic on the Fourth of July. This became a yearly event and people would come from all over the area. The men would have a parade before hand to advertise the picnic, promote the department, and look for new volunteers and donations.

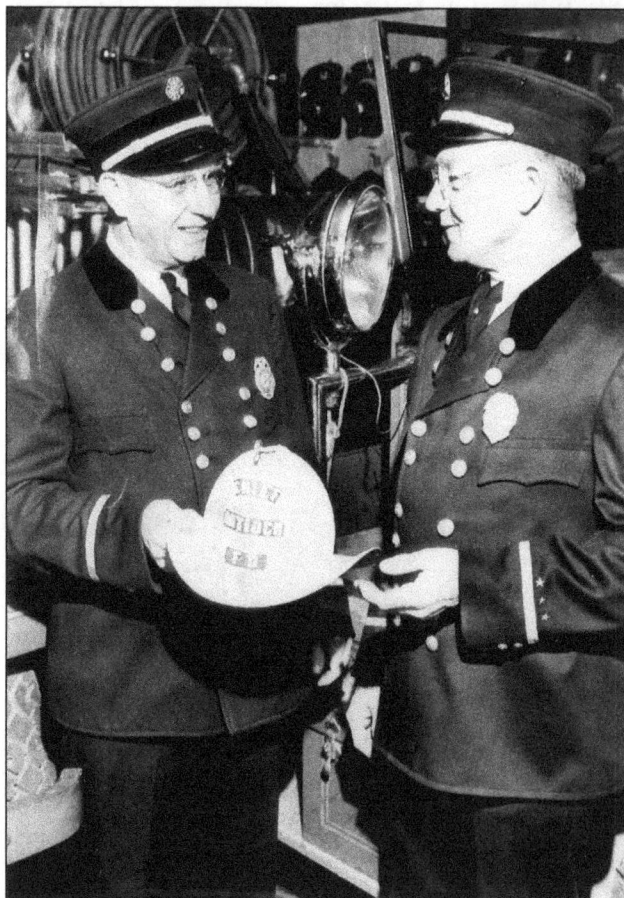

Louis Van Patten (right), who had been fire chief since 1941, passes the hat to Clete Vos (left) in 1946. Jim McMillen (not pictured) was assistant chief under Vos and would become mayor in 1950. The department celebrated its 40th anniversary in 1953. Van Patten was the only charter member still alive at the time. When the department formed in 1913 it had 28 charter members.

By the late 1930s it was obvious that the fire department needed more space. In 1940, the village took bids to build a new safety building for the fire department. This photograph shows the result. The police department was on the east side of this state-of-the-art building at Orchard Street and Toft Avenue. (Courtesy of the Village of Antioch.)

The Antioch Lions Club was formed in 1937 and one of their projects was to get a rescue squad for the community. Fund-raising began, and by May 1940 almost $900 had been raised. Then they began raising funds to build a building next to the fire station. They raised over $18,000 by 1952 when the building was completed.

The bay window in this photograph is the office of Dr. Harry Beebe. He was the local health officer, and in 1919 when the flu epidemic struck the Antioch area, it was his responsibility to take action. He closed all the schools, churches, and any gathering place in order to curb the spread. Two other town doctors helped him and together they cared for over 300 people, including several who died. This photograph was probably taken around 1900. The community of Antioch would have never survived without the dedication and commitment of the hundreds, no thousands, of people who lived here. It is because of the people that this community did not go the way of so many little towns from the 1800s. So many faded into history but Antioch has that spark, that something special that gives it life. Little did the Gage brothers know, when they settled along the Sequoit Creek, what they would create.

Five

ALL AROUND THE TOWN

The people of Antioch have always had one thing in common. They like to have fun. Parades, celebrations, parties, good food, and good times are part of every-day life in the community. This parade from the 1920s was only the beginning. The streets had been paved in 1920 creating a much smoother ride for the revelers. The flat-bed trucks were perfect for floats. Parades happen in town for Easter, Fourth of July, homecoming, and Christmas and the occasional special event. The Fourth of July celebration has it roots all the way back to 1839 when it was reported that the early settlers took that day to celebrate the founding of the country. They got together for a meal and read the Declaration of Independence and shot off their guns. Ever since then this community has celebrated that most special day. A fabulous parade, great food, and games at Williams Park and the best fireworks display happen every Fourth in Antioch.

The hotel was built in 1850 by Davis R. Gage. At some point he sold it to J. B. Rice who then sold it to Levi J. Simons in April 1882. When Ernest L. Simons assumed ownership from his father, he held a partnership with F. C. Sabin. In September 1905 the partnership was dissolved and Ernest Simons assumed total ownership. The hotel was the center of activity around town for many years.

The location of the Simons Hotel was at the now southwest corner of Main Street and Orchard Street. Levi J. Simons added a large brick addition on the north side that included a hall for large events. Everything from dances, to funerals and town meetings, weddings, parties, and lectures would take place there. Note the livery stable at the rear of the hotel.

Elegant invitations would go out to the important people in town. What fun to go to a masquerade ball and dance the evening away. Glowing lights, music by the Wilson Band, and a wonderful supper made for a Cinderella evening for any young lady. All this for only $1.75.

Yourself and Ladies are cordially invited to attend a

MASQUERADE BALL,

—AT—

SIMON'S HALL,

Antioch, Illinois.

—ON—

Thursday Eve., February 22, 1883.

Floor Managers,

T. A. EMMONS, Monaville,   H. HORTON, Antioch,

BEN. HOYSRADT, Salem.

Music by Wilson's Full Band.   Tickets, Including Supper, $1.75.

The Simons Hotel served the community for 89 years. In 1929, there was a rumor that the hotel would be replaced by a new, modern facility but that did not happen. By April 1939 the building was torn down. The village board hoped for, and got, federal funds to help build a village hall on the site. (Courtesy of Thomas and Catherine [Bogan] Middlebrook.)

Lyman Grice built his hotel in 1891 just north of the Simons Hotel. Today it would be the northwest corner of Orchard Street and Main Street. The building had 22 rooms to accommodate the people coming out to the lakes for vacation and for the traveling businessmen. Archie Maplethorpe's horse-drawn carriage on the left would later be placed on a 1914 Ford chassis.

The hotel continued to serve the community for many years, and after an addition, some new paint, and modern conveniences, it morphed into this building. Grice had sold the hotel to Arthur Edgar, who sold to Charles Lux in 1902, who sold to Barney Naber, who later sold it to Chris Mortensen in 1942. In 1966 it was sold and was demolished in 1967 to make way for a modern service station of the Phillips Petroleum Company.

There is confusion over when the Crystal Theatre building was actually built. But it is believed to have been between 1916 and 1919. This theater served a dual purpose as it could show motion pictures and also had a stage for vaudeville acts including the Rottner Players. It continued to show movies well into the 1950s. In the 1960s, the building started housing the Palette, Masque and Lyre Theater group. They have been presenting live performances since then.

The Antioch Theatre started out as the Barney F. Nabor Store, and in 1919 it was remodeled into a modern movie theater. The Majestic Theater moved in, and in July they bought two new reel machines so that a movie could be watched without interruption. The name changed to the Antioch Theatre sometime in the 1930s and has remained so since.

Imagine bumping along this road to get to the Channel Lake Pavilion and several other resorts on Lake Catherine, Channel Lake, and Lake Marie. This scenic route would eventually become Route 173 heading west of town. Sections of it were moved to accommodate building growth but it is basically in the same location today. (Courtesy of Thomas and Catherine [Bogan] Middlebrook.)

The Channel Lake Pavilion had a long history of fires and rebuilding. The first pavilion, pictured here, was built sometime late in the second decade of the 20th century. The early buildings were not built to withstand the harsh winters. In 1924, a new pavilion was built, and this one was converted into apartments. Unfortunately the entire building burned in 1935 causing $6,000 in damage.

The new Channel Lake Pavilion was beautiful. Larger and better built, it had everything that the vacationer and the local people wanted. An early advertisement stated "greatest line of attractions under any one roof—our friends advertise us, 'nuff said." There was dancing every night, not just on the weekends.

The dance floor was the largest in the entire area. It really was the social gathering place in the 1920s. Even when the Depression started, the pavilion was still a place to go to relieve the pressures that people had in their lives. It only lasted until 1933 when it burned to the ground. In 1941, T. J. Palaske bought what was left and demolished it for the lumber that had been saved.

The Channel Lake Country Club and golf course was completed in 1924 and brought a new attraction to the Antioch area. This growing popular sport had a clubhouse where guests could stay and get up early to be on the course. It was located on Country Club Drive off Route 173 about four miles west of town. The clubhouse is still there, although now it is a private residence.

An advertisement in the *Antioch News* in June 1951 boasted that the Chain 'O Lakes Country Club (established in 1920) was the Lakes Region's most outstanding golf course. Rates were weekdays $1.50, twilight 75¢ and Saturdays $2, twilight $1. This club was purchased by George Diamond in 1955. (Courtesy of Thomas and Catherine [Bogan] Middlebrook.)

The toboggan slide was completed in January 1940 at Lake Antioch. Starting with the gentleman in the fireman hat, from left to right are Clete Vos, Jim McMillian, unidentified, Herman Holbeck, and Jim Steans. The firemen brought the truck out to pump water down the slide to make it slide easier. This winter sport was enjoyed by many.

Summertime brought the players and spectators alike to the ballpark next to the library. Adult baseball had always been a favorite, and the children needed a place to play also. Baseball is still a major sporting event in the area.

This restaurant was built during the 1920s along Route 83 south of town. Although it has changed hands and names, the building has withstood the test of time. Always a restaurant, the fare changed sometimes but it was always good. Some names to remember are Arnie's Roundup, Ruralite, Tony and Lil's, Avanti, J. T. Roadhouse, U Genes, and the current Johnny's Chop House.

F. Wohlfeil's Tavern off Grass Lake Road at Rena Avenue has quenched the thirst of many a traveler in its day. A great place to stop either on the way out to the resorts or on the way home from work, it has never stopped serving guests. It is now J. D. Bootleggers and continues to be a great place to stop for a wet one. (Courtesy of Thomas and Catherine [Bogan] Middlebrook.)

This early home, built in 1852 by Elijah Simmons, sat high on the hill. It was passed on to his son Frank and then on to Frank's son-in-law William Smart. Mary Simmons Smart ran a boardinghouse for some time before she sold the farm to Bernie Haviland, who turned it into a restaurant and in turn sold it to Ray and Gert Lorenz.

Look very closely at the section of the building with two stories, and compare it with the photograph above. With some remodeling and updating and additions the old Simmons farmhouse became the well known Lorenz's Smart Country House. Many residents will remember the elegant dining and wonderful entertainment that it provided. Today Country Pontiac sits atop the hill and still has a little of the Simmon/Smart home in it.

Joe and Helen Sterbenz's Nielsen's Corners was on the northwest corner of Grass Lake Road and Route 59. Travelers could stop and get the best barbecue ribs in the county. Do not like ribs, how about baked ham? The menu held something for every taste. Need gas for the car? That was provided also. Then the traveler was ready for the rest of his trip. Locals made this a stop also.

Small stores popped up everywhere in the resort area. Since travel was not always the easiest and there were no large grocery stores like today, the need for these stores was great. This one was probably along Lake Avenue in the Channel Lake area. The bus is really great. (Courtesy of Thomas and Catherine [Bogan] Middlebrook.)

The Channel Lake Boat House sat right along Route 173 by the bridge over the channel between Channel Lake and Lake Marie. With that location they could provide all the same amenities that the other little stores had and add the incentive of boats for rent. Park the car, rent a boat, and spend the day fishing on the lakes. Now that is the way to relax. Webb's Boathouse sits here now.

This was A. Wolf's store and hotel on Loon Lake. It was built in 1907 and this photograph is from the 1930s. The lady in the center is Barbara Hoffmann Wolf. Her husband Andrew was the proprietor, but it was probably Barbara that kept the place in order. S.O.S. Well Drilling is located here now. (Courtesy of Pam Martz)

The first Eugene Cox store actually stood right on the shore of Channel Lake. At that time, the road passed right in front of the store. When Route 173 was opened up in 1935 to go between Zion and Richmond, sections of it moved. Because the road was now a distance from the store, Cox made the decision to move the store also. (Courtesy of Thomas and Catherine [Bogan] Middlebrook.)

When Cox moved the store, he expanded the business to include a tavern and more gas pumps. He stilled carried groceries, ice cream, and the like but business really grew. It became known to the locals as well as travelers as Cox's Corners because of its location on a corner. The building is still there and still is a tavern. (Courtesy of Thomas and Catherine [Bogan] Middlebrook.)

The Antioch Palace was built by Richard Macek in 1926–1927. It was located south on Route 83 near the area of Beach Grove Road. The 125-foot-by-180-foot building boasted that it would include bowling alleys, pool tables, soda fountain, lunch counter, check room, and a 20-foot-by-95-foot dance floor. A total of 5,000 people can be comfortable inside while there will be parking for over 1,000 cars. Even a filling station would be included.

The palace opened in April 1927 to the music of the Floridians Orchestra. Amateur boxing occurred every Friday night and even some professional boxers came in. All this splendor lasted only three years, as the palace burned in 1929.

The Smith Hotel and Resort was one of the most popular in the area. The property was right on the south shore of Channel Lake. Guests must have been swimming as there are several bathing suits laid over the railing to dry. The hotel was destroyed by an overnight fire in November 1927.

The dining room served meals family style and these young women would make a very good salary during the summer months. A competent girl could demand as much as $5 or $6 per week. These young ladies would have all been single as a married woman would have been home taking care of her house and family.

What marvelous fun! When the lakes were formed by the Wisconsin glacier thousands of years ago, in several places there were high bluffs left such as this one. The slides were put in for the enjoyment of the guests. Although many of the older guests would choose to walk down the stairs, most of the younger ones would take the swift way down.

There were not only two separate hotels on the property but many cottages as well. These cottages could be rented by the day, week, or even the entire summer. Families would come out from the city and while mother and children would stay, the father would commute on the train every weekend. In later years, these families would build summer homes and eventually permanent ones. (Courtesy of Thomas and Catherine [Bogan] Middlebrook.)

The Ball Game, Queen of the West Hotel, Petite Lake, Antioch, Ill. 8242-r

The Queen of the West Hotel on Petite Lake was by far one of the most popular. As seen in this postcard, the hotel was very large and most of these people where certainly staying there. It looks like an impromptu ball game is underway and the ladies are cheering on their men. No doubt some of the locals were in on the game also. The hotel was opened in April 1893 by Albert Hermann.

This view of the Queen of the West is from the lakeside. It sits atop one of those bluffs and has a very wide stair going down to the water. Small boats would be available for the guests to take out for a row, and on the shore is a large tour boat that would be used to take guests to view the lotus beds in Grass Lake. This may have been after the season so the boat has been pulled onto the land. (Courtesy of Thomas and Catherine [Bogan] Middlebrook.)

Ira M. Simons had his hotel on the shores of Petite Lake. This hotel was referred to as the Petite Lake Hotel and also as the Simon's Hotel. The building in the foreground would be used for evening entertainment. The lake was behind the hotel on the hill. (Courtesy of Thomas and Catherine [Bogan] Middlebrook.)

Dressel's Resort was on the southeast shore of Lake Marie. Here are several guests arriving for a vacation. They actually look like they are ready for a great time. The Dressel's was known for catering to the first-class families and Matilda Dressel's reputation for home cooking was stellar.

This photograph of Rhymer's at Loon Lake is an excellent example of how families would add on to the home and open up as a hotel. The guests would be fed with the family. This was probably in the early fall, as the summer guests were gone but the hunters and fishermen were still coming out from the city.

Savage's Pavilion on Channel Lake sat right at the water's edge. This is an early picture, and in a few years, an addition would be made to accommodate larger crowds. In 1905, Joseph Savage purchased a building in town so that he could tear it down and use the lumber to build cottages on the lake property. (Courtesy of Thomas and Catherine [Bogan] Middlebrook.)

Selter's Resort on Grass Lake was a favorite among the hunters and fishermen. The fish hanging on the building would have been a one-day catch. These able men have all posed with their rifles. Should there be concern for the safety of the duck posing with them?

Rother's Resort on Grass Lake was a well-rounded place. In the summer, the pavilion provided a meeting place for the adults while the children played on the sandy beach. Butch Rother was known for his experience in hunting, and after the summer season, he would cater to the fall hunters.

Shannon's Pavilion and swimming beach was especially popular with the locals. Once school was out, the children would head for the water. Before the motorboats took over the lakes, the water was clear and sparkling and wonderful for swimming.

Steitz's Resort on Bluff Lake is still in business today. Started as a hunting and fishing resort, today it is well known for its restaurant and marina. This photograph is from 1938.

Opened in 1906, the Ray Pregenzer place catered to the hunters also. His hotel was heated so the hunters could warm up quickly upon a return from a day of hunting. Mr. Haling was a frequent guest and decided to open his own resort next to Pregenzer's. Eventually he bought out Pregenzer and made that property part of Halings Resort. Halings is still in business today as a marina. (Courtesy of Thomas and Catherine [Bogan] Middlebrook.)

The Sylvan Beach Hotel on Channel Lake had one of the most elegant dining rooms in the area. Not only the guests enjoyed the wonderful meals, but the locals frequented the dining room also. The Sylvan dated back to the 1890s. The hotel had a very large veranda with many rocking chairs for the comfort of the guests.

Bluff Lake was home to the Jurchik Resort. The people in this photograph were probably guests of the hotel or maybe family. The back of the picture says that the third person from the left is John Jurchik, proprietor of the resort. The date is probably about 1915.

Herman's Lawn on Bluff Lake was a lovely place. This 1890s photograph shows the wide spaces between cabins creating a quiet atmosphere. The ladies seem to be very relaxed and enjoying themselves.

Summer Home near Simon's Hotel, Petite Lake 385 Antioch Ill

As people fell in love with the area, many built summer homes so they would always have a place to stay. Most of these homes would eventually be made permanent with the addition of heating systems and indoor plumbing. Although the lots were very inexpensive in the 1890s, today's prices reflect the popularity of lake property. (Courtesy of Thomas and Catherine [Bogan] Middlebrook.)

The ever-popular Blarney's Island is still hopping today. The "Island" used to be connected to land, but when the McHenry dam was constructed, the lake levels rose and now it is indeed an island. It served as a viewing point for looking at the fabulous lotus beds of Grass Lake. Today Blarney's Island, with a tavern and boat races, is a hotspot in the summer, catering to the young adults.

A BUNCH OF LOTUS. GRASS LAKE ANTIOCH ILL.

The lotus beds on Grass Lake were known far and wide. Although it is widely believed that these lotus are only found here and in Egypt, they have been found in other locations. It was probably the Native Americans in this area that first planted them as the seed pods were a food product for them. Once the lotus covered the lakes like a carpet. But when the white man found the Chain O' Lakes area the lotus all but disappeared. The people picked the beautiful flowers, the motorboats churned up the delicate beds, and the worse destruction was the McHenry Dam that raised the water level above the height of the plant. The plants are rooted in the lake bottom and must reach the sunlight to bloom. Fortunately a few plants remained, and in the late summer, small beds can be found along some of the shorelines where the water is shallow. More information can be found on the resorts and the lakes in *Chain O' Lakes* by the authors.

Six

CONTINUED GROWTH

The 1950s and 1960s brought new growth to the Antioch area. The troops who had returned home from World War II were anxious to start new lives. There were stoplights at Lake Street and Main Street and parking meters in town. The buildings looked the same but the businesses were different. The schools had to add space or build new buildings. The high school had over 1,000 students. New churches came to town to service the spiritual needs of the growing population. There was new lighting for the downtown street that made it feel like daylight. House to house postal delivery finally became a reality, the post office finally got a permanent home, and Antioch got a postal zone (60002). The telephone became a direct dial and used seven digits. A mastodon bone was found in the industrial area that is said to be between 6,000 and 12,000 years old. So humans were not the first ones here. The banks in town put in drive-through banking. In 1968, the Antioch Sequoit Football team, under the coaching of Roy Nelson, brought home the conference championship after a 26 years drought. (Courtesy of the Village of Antioch.)

The Antioch Evangelical Free Church broke ground for a building on October 1, 1961. Over the years they have ministered to many and the church has grown rapidly. Now called the Crossview Church it is on Tiffany Road. (Courtesy of the Village of Antioch.)

St. Stephens Lutheran Church on the hill laid their cornerstone in September 1967. The Reverend L. A. Anderson performed the ceremony. When the church was dedicated in December of the same year, Wilton J. Anderson was pastor. (Courtesy of the Village of Antioch.)

Here is a great photograph of the first drive-through facility for the First National Bank. The bank had moved into this larger building in 1966 when the State Bank of Antioch built a new facility on Lake Street. In 1972, the First National Bank would build a new facility across the street from the State Bank of Antioch. (Courtesy of the Village of Antioch.)

To supply housing for the people moving out from the city, developers first started building apartment buildings. This provided housing for those people who were making transitions or just starting out. Housing developments, not unlike the subdivisions that had been built in the 1920s, would continue. The boundaries of the village started to swell outward. (Courtesy of the Village of Antioch.)

John Teresi Chevy-Olds was one of the most popular car dealerships around. The dealership is now owned by Raymond Scarpelli and is located on Route 173. But this original building was on Main Street at Orchard Street. The village bought the property when the dealership moved and tore it down to make room for an extension to Orchard Street. The traffic pattern changed and once a stoplight was added it made a huge difference. (Courtesy of the Village of Antioch.)

The Orchard Plaza was conceived in 1962, and the A&P became the anchor store on the east and Ace Hardware on the west. The A&P grand opening was in February 1965, and it was the first store there. Just one year later it was destroyed by fire. It was rebuilt and reopened in October 1966. (Courtesy of the Village of Antioch.)

The Fillweber and Wilton properties were purchased in 1955 for the Jewel Food store. A 1960 advertisement was for pot roast at 39¢ a pound and heads of lettuce at 10¢ each. In 1966, an addition was put on to increase the size of the store. Several years later, the Jewel Food burned in an overnight fire, and the company decided not to rebuild on that site. The new store was built at the current site. (Courtesy of the Village of Antioch.)

Thompson's Grill at 933 Main Street was a mainstay in the community for 40 years. Ralph Thompson provided a wonderful meal. Lines would form waiting to get into the restaurant. Then, what appears to be an Antioch curse, fire struck. In just a few hours, the entire building was reduced to rubble. Not wanting to rebuild, the property is now a little walk-through park.

The people of Antioch have always enjoyed entertainment and fun. The carnival still comes to town in the summer. This photograph is from the weekend of August 12, 13, and 14, 1938. It was held on the location that is now Toft Avenue before it was a street.

A summertime event that began in the later 1970s and still takes place today is the Lions Club Bar-B-Q Chicken Dinner and auction to benefit the Antioch Rescue Squad. The monies raised at this annual event benefit the work of the Lions Club and helps support the vital volunteer rescue squad. There are usually great deals to be found at the auction.

When Ted Larson was president of the Lions Club in 1954 he wanted to see a pool built in Antioch. Several dedicated Lions went to work, and by July 1956 the pool was a reality. Over the years, the pool was eventually turned over to the village and the Antioch Parks and Recreations Department now oversees its running. (Courtesy of the Village of Antioch.)

Summer craft fairs have become an expected event in Antioch. Starting on a very small scale with just a few artisans the June and September craft fairs have blossomed into mega events. How many of these paintings might still be hanging in an Antioch house today? (Courtesy of the Village of Antioch.)

Pickard China Company is probably the best known business in Antioch. The company was founded in 1897, but it was not until 1937 that they came to Antioch. They purchased the Corona Pen factory and later the street name changed from Corona Street to Pickard Avenue. By 1941, they moved the entire operation from Chicago out to the Antioch site. The exquisite china is still being made in Antioch. (Courtesy of the Village of Antioch.)

The Frostee Sno Company began in Antioch on Main Street, but by the 1960s they needed to build a new modern facility and chose a site in the fairly new industrial park on the east side of town. In 1962, the plant was ready to go. John and Wanda Oftedahl were the owners. Although the company is no longer in business, some of the products they made can be seen in the "Made in Antioch" display at the Lake Region Historical Society's Meeting House Museum at 977 Main Street.

Quaker Industries, a house wares manufacturer from Kenosha, Wisconsin, decided to relocate to Antioch in 1961. This facility on Anita Street in the industrial park no longer houses Quaker, but as with Frostee Sno, products made here are on display at the Lake Region Historical Society's Meeting House Museum. (Courtesy of the Village of Antioch.)

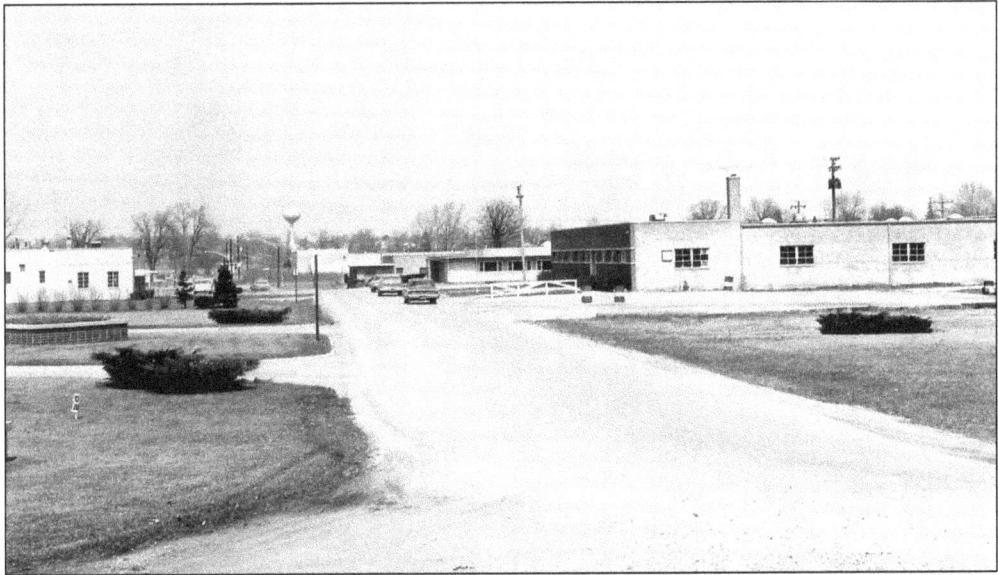

Chicago Ink and Research was the first company to build in Sequoit Industrial acres in 1955. By 1965, they added a 4,200 square foot addition. The industrial park is on the east side of town and Anita Street is the main road through. Most of the factories are between Ida Avenue and Depot Street. (Courtesy of the Village of Antioch.)

The Gambles Store at 952 Main Street was a staple in town. If someone needed a new stove they went to see Rudy Eckert, the owner. His store supplied all the things needed for home repairs and improvements. Look closely at the south side of the building today and the faded *Gambles* is still visible.

The Antioch Bowling building went up in 1953 with 12 lanes. A later addition expanded that to 20 lanes. Bowling has been a favorite sport in Antioch every since the Golwitzer's Barber Shop had two lanes on the second floor back in the early 1920s. (Courtesy of the Village of Antioch.)

Dr. Albert Bucar was far more than the local optometrist. He was extremely active in the community. He had followed in the footsteps of the other doctors of all kinds. Prior to Bucar, this was the office of Dr. Irving Breakstone and Dr. James Kopriva. When Breakstone left the practice, Dr. Alan Thain joined. This little white house still stands on Orchard Street. (Courtesy of the Village of Antioch.)

The town of Antioch is a very special and unique place to be. There is no place else quite like it. It changes constantly yet stays the same. It is still a place where people help people, where everyone is a neighbor even though the names are not the same. It is a privilege to call Antioch home.

ACROSS AMERICA, PEOPLE ARE DISCOVERING
SOMETHING WONDERFUL. THEIR HERITAGE.

Arcadia Publishing is the leading local history publisher in the United States.
With more than 3,000 titles in print and hundreds of new titles released every
year, Arcadia has extensive specialized experience chronicling the history of
communities and celebrating America's hidden stories, bringing to life the people,
places, and events from the past. To discover the history of other communities
across the nation, please visit:

www.arcadiapublishing.com

Customized search tools allow you to find regional history books about the town
where you grew up, the cities where your friends and family live, the town where
your parents met, or even that retirement spot you've been dreaming about.

www.ingramcontent.com/pod-product-compliance
Lightning Source LLC
Chambersburg PA
CBHW080549110426
42813CB00006B/1255